MINI M...

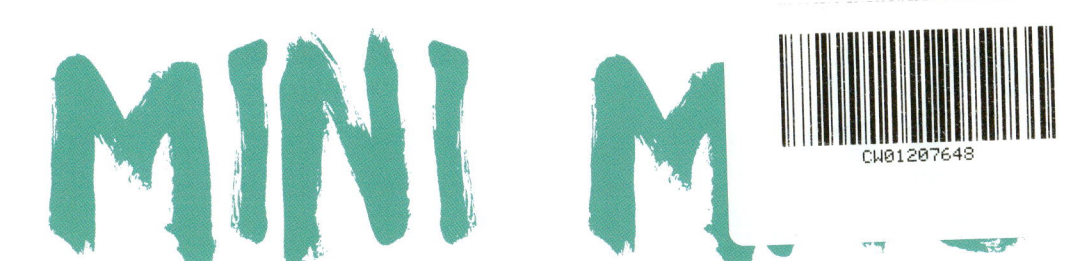

THE MONSTER UNDERNEATH MY BED

Mini Mac
The Monster Underneath My Bed

All rights reserved; no part of this publication may be reproduced or transmitted by any means, electronic, mechanical, photocopying or otherwise, without the prior permission of the publisher.

Published by Katie Pendrigh

Written by Katie Pendrigh

Illustrations and book design by
Glen Holman (www.glenholman.com)

ISBN: 978-1-9161644-0-6

Copyright © Katie Pendrigh 2019
The moral right of the author has been asserted.
A CIP catalogue record of this book is available from the British Library

MINI MAC

THE MONSTER UNDERNEATH MY BED

Written by **KATIE PENDRIGH**
Illustrated by **GLEN HOLMAN**

For Eddie and Rosie.

And my own Best Friend, Ange.

There is a mini monster who lives underneath my bed.

I often hear him playing whilst I rest my sleepy head.

I'm not at all scared of him, there is no need to be.

For all he really wants is to be a friend to me.

His name is Mac the Monster, his eyes are strangely green.

He has tall pointy ears and a big nose in between.

His feet are very tiny, his knees have lots of hair.

He does not look too pretty but he really doesn't care.

Sometimes he will laugh and laugh,
rolling around the floor.

He'll find little things so funny and
laugh a little more.

He once performed a show,
where he sang a silly song.

I've never heard him laugh so much
when the end went wrong.

And if I am ever sad, he will often say to me.

'Don't pull that funny face, it makes you look a bit silly.'

If ever I am in my room and feeling rather down.

He comes and sits beside me and turns my frown upside down.

He really is becoming
a very good friend of mine.

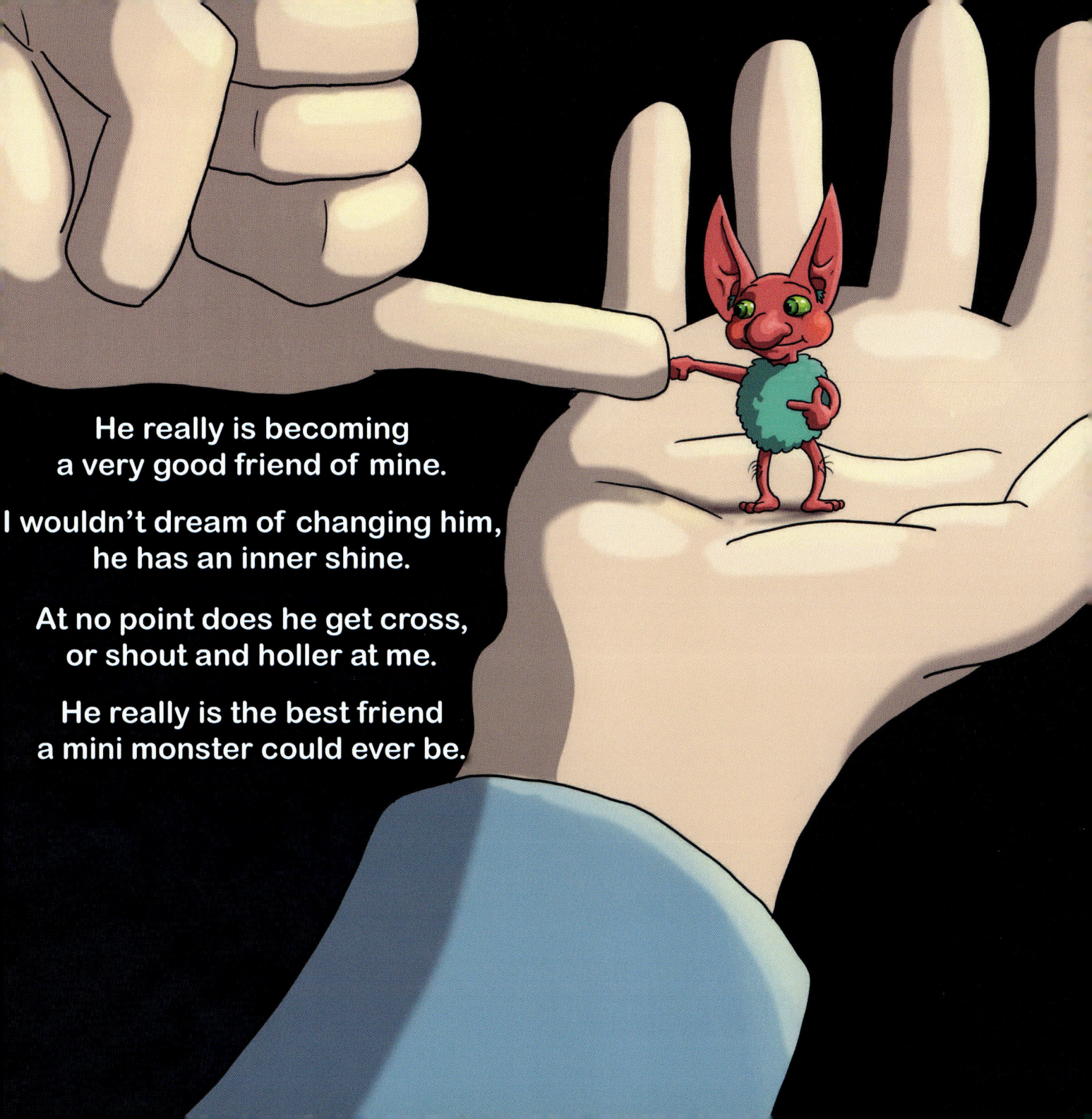

I wouldn't dream of changing him,
he has an inner shine.

At no point does he get cross,
or shout and holler at me.

He really is the best friend
a mini monster could ever be.

One night whilst I was sleeping,
Mac got up upon my chair.

Awoke me with a startle,
I heard him roar; now that was rare.

He said it was his birthday
and a party was to be had.

He wanted to invite his family
and introduce me to his dad.

So a party I threw him
and it was so great.

It started at my bedtime
and nobody was late.

I'd sneaked up cheese and sausages
for everyone to share.

Chocolate cakes and fruity drinks
that tasted just like pear.

Everyone was laughing lots
and having real good fun.

It was all so exciting
yet had only just begun.

We played silly games,
sang songs and danced all night.

And it wasn't till the end that we
all got quite a fright.

Just as we were playing
mini monster musical bumps.

I landed on my bottom
and made a loud thump.

We stopped what we were doing,
I crept slowly to the door.

When suddenly a footstep could
be heard on the landing floor.

All the monsters ran
underneath my bed to hide.

The party was all over,
I really could have cried.

It was my mum to check on me,
"What's all this noise about?

I heard loud noises, a thump
and lots of people shout".

"I do not know", I said to mum,
"I've been so fast asleep,

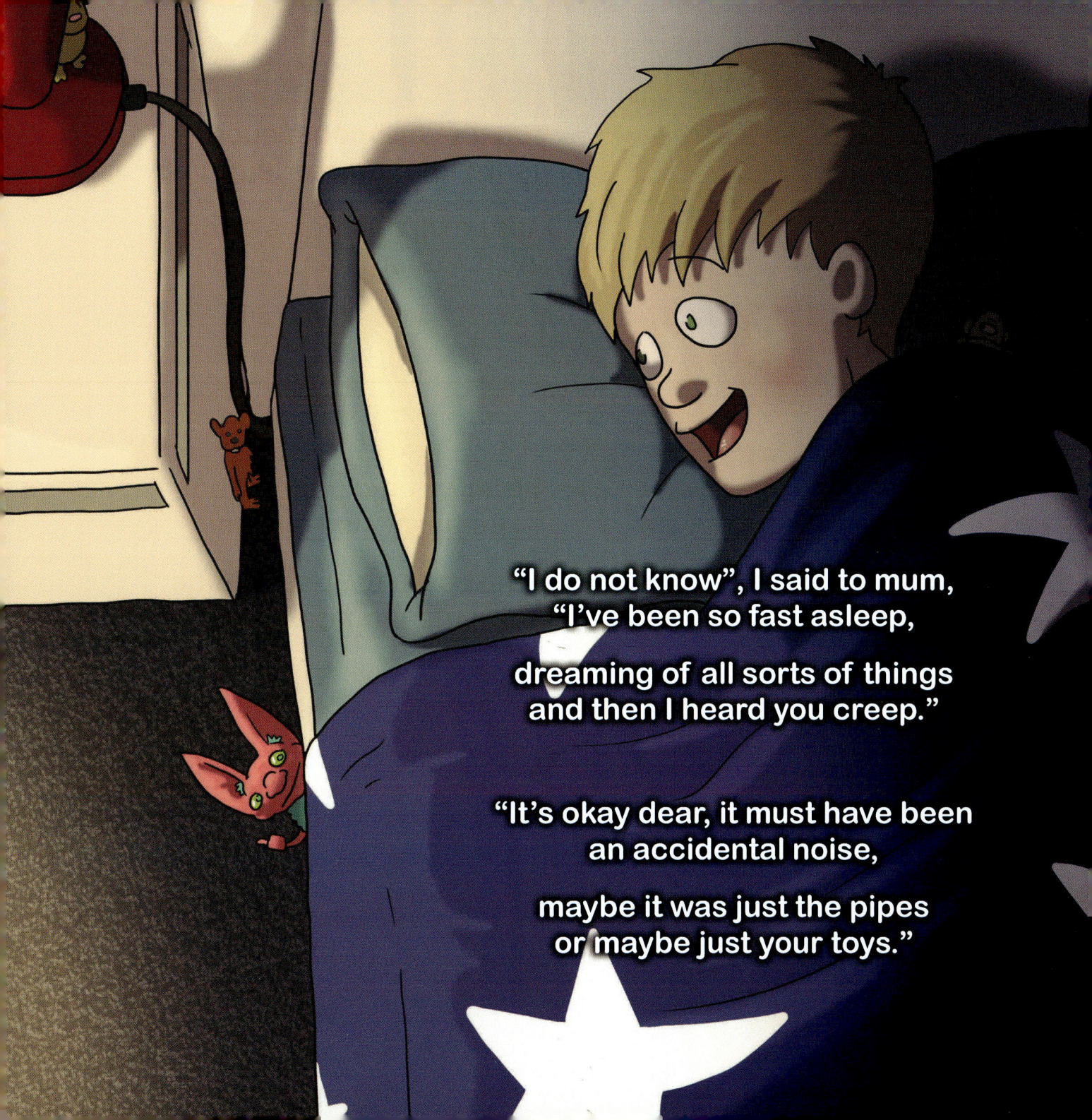

dreaming of all sorts of things
and then I heard you creep."

"It's okay dear, it must have been
an accidental noise,

maybe it was just the pipes
or maybe just your toys."

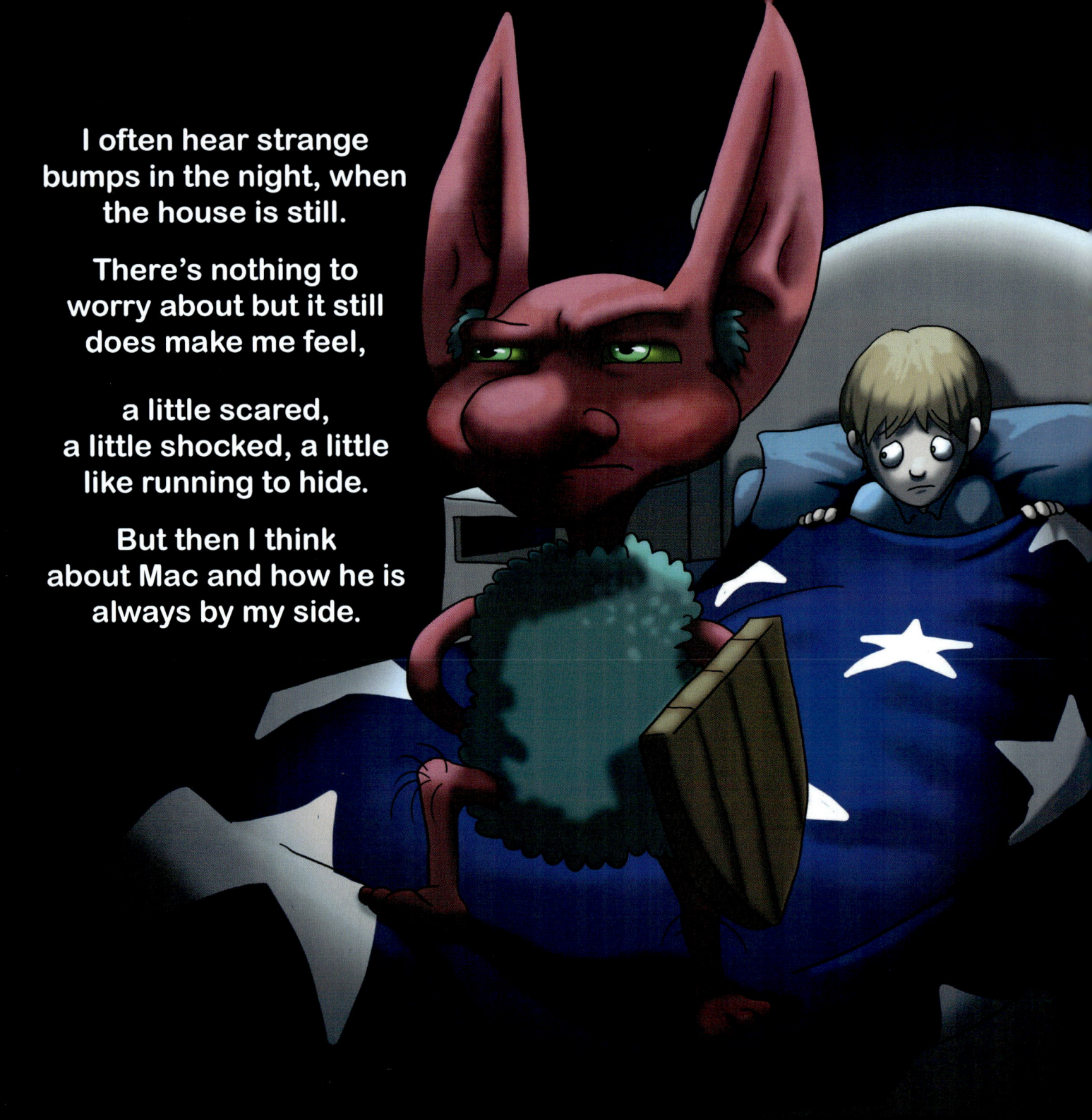

I often hear strange bumps in the night, when the house is still.

There's nothing to worry about but it still does make me feel,

a little scared,
a little shocked, a little like running to hide.

But then I think about Mac and how he is always by my side.

My mum went back downstairs,
the mini monsters all crept out.

There was Mac, his mum and dad
and his friends all stood about.

They thanked me for the party
and said they'd had a lovely time.

They were looking forward to next
year's when Mac would be turning nine.

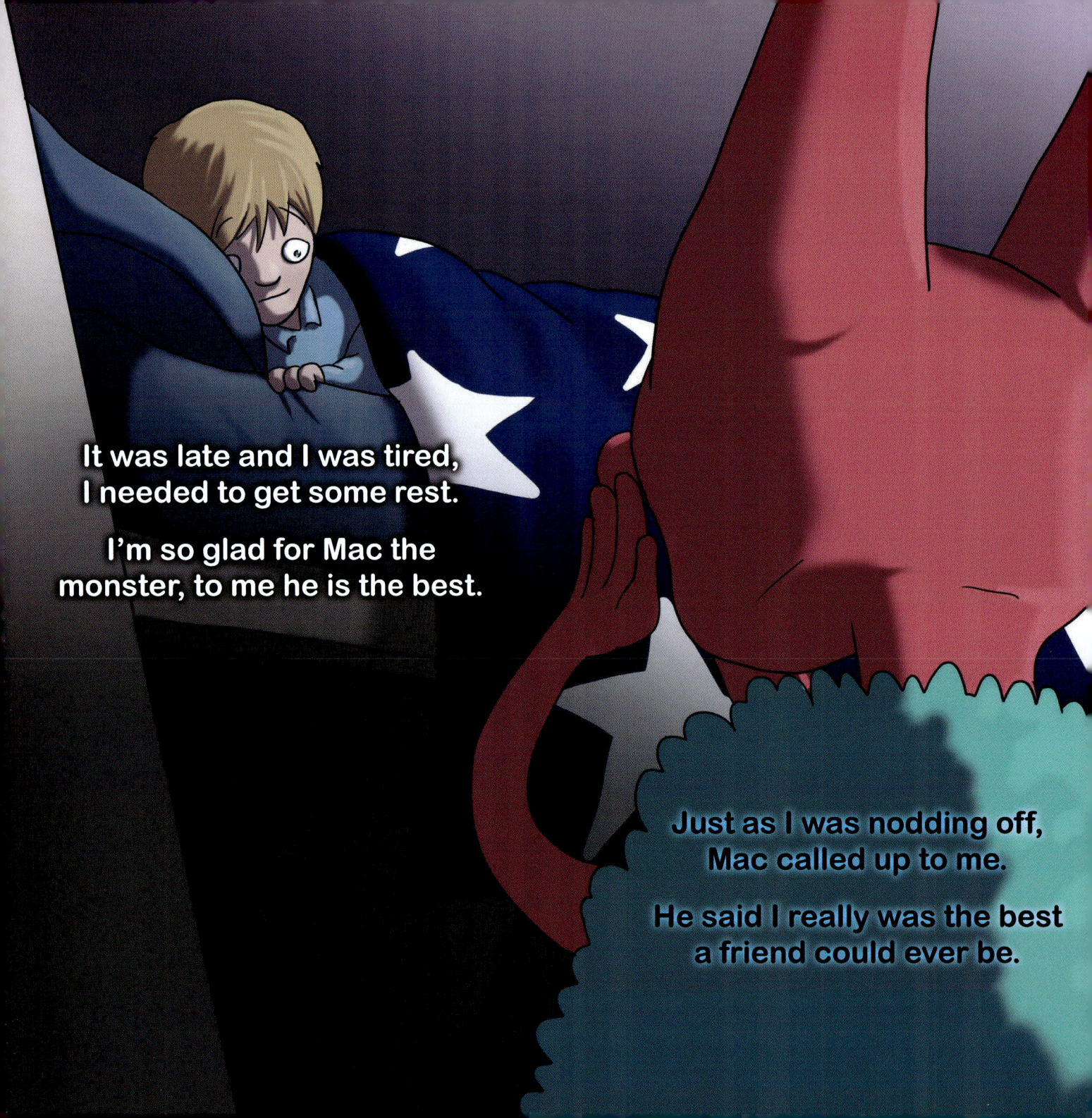

It was late and I was tired, I needed to get some rest.

I'm so glad for Mac the monster, to me he is the best.

Just as I was nodding off, Mac called up to me.

He said I really was the best a friend could ever be.

I'm glad that I'm a good friend, it's so very important to be.

Kind, caring and sharing, then my friends will be the same to me.

Friends are really good to have,
friends are really great.

Everyone should have one,
a very special mate.